The Months of School

by Margie Sigman

 Harcourt

SCHOOL PUBLISHERS

Orlando   Austin   New York   San Diego   Toronto   London

Visit *The Learning Site!*
www.harcourtschool.com

Fall

Winter

Spring

Summer

September days are hot.

We wear short sleeves.

It's the first day of school!

October days are windy.

The leaves fall. The colors change.

We wear jackets to play outside.

November days are chilly.

The days are short. It gets dark early.

At school we exercise.

December days are snowy.

We wear warm boots and mittens.

At school we play in the snow.

January days are icy.

The ground is hard and slippery.

At school we play inside.

February days are cold.

When will spring come?

At school we read our books.

March days are windy.

Spring is in the air!

At school we climb and swing.

April days are rainy.

The ground is wet and squishy.

At school we build with blocks.

May days are sunny.

The flowers bloom. The birds sing.

At school we act silly.

June days are warm.

The trees are green again.

At school we say good-bye, because . . .

it's summertime!